This book is t
the las

My Day

Siobhan Dodds

W

FRANKLIN WATTS

LONDON•SYDNEY

Every morning I get dressed —
sometimes I need help.

I eat bread and jam for breakfast.

Then it's time to go to school.

Today, we sing and dance.

We paint pictures and build.

When I get home I feed my rabbit.

After tea I splash in the bath.

Then it's time for bed.

car

bath

jam

T-shirt

clock

book

rabbit

bricks

Sharing books with your child

Early Worms are a range of books for you to share with your child. Together you can look at the pictures and talk about the subject or story. Listening, looking and talking are the first vital stages in children's reading development, and lay the early foundation for good reading habits.

Talking about the pictures is the first step in involving children in the pages of a book, especially if the subject or story can be related to their own familiar world. When children can relate the matter in the book to their own experience, this can be used as a starting point for introducing new knowledge, whether it is counting, getting to know colours or finding out how other people live.

Gradually children will develop their listening and concentration skills as well as a sense of what a book is. Soon they will learn how a book works: that you turn the pages from right to left, and read the story from left to right on a double page. They start to realize that the black marks on the page have a meaning and that they relate to the pictures. Once children have grasped these basic essentials they will develop strategies for "decoding" the text such as matching words and pictures, and recognising the rhythm of the language in order to predict what comes next. Soon they will start to take on the role of an independent reader, handling and looking at books even if they can't yet read the words.

Most important of all, children should realize that books are a source of pleasure. This stems from your reading sessions which are times of mutual enjoyment and shared experience. It is then that children find the key to becoming real readers.

© 1998 Siobhan Dodds
(Text and Illustrations)

This edition published in 2001 by

Franklin Watts
96 Leonard Street
London EC2A 4XD

Franklin Watts Australia
56 O'Riordan Street
Alexandria, Sydney, NSW 2015

ISBN 0 7496 3516 9

A CIP catalogue record for this book
is available from the British Library.

Series Editor: Paula Borton
Art Director: Robert Walster
Photographer: Steve Shott
With thanks to Ben Ridley-Johnson

Printed in Belgium

Consultant advice: Sue Robson and Alison Kelly, Senior Lecturers in Education,
Faculty of Education, Early Childhood Centre, Roehampton Institute, London.